100 Interesting Facts About Guatemala

A Collection of Amazing Facts About Guatemala

Introduction

Welcome to "100 Interesting Facts About Guatemala for Young Readers!" Get ready to explore a country of ancient ruins, colorful markets, and stunning landscapes. Discover how Guatemala's rich history and vibrant culture make it a truly amazing place. Each page is packed with fascinating facts about Guatemala's landmarks, traditions, and wildlife. Dive in and start your adventure today!

Chapter 1 : Places to Visit

- Fact 1: Lake Atitlán

- Fact 2: Tikal National Park

- Fact 3: Antigua Guatemala

- Fact 4: Semuc Champey

- Fact 5: Chichicastenango Market

Fact 1: Lake Atitlán

Lake Atitlán is a stunningly beautiful highland lake surrounded by three majestic volcanoes: Atitlán, San Pedro, and Tolimán. Located in the Guatemalan highlands, it's renowned for its breathtaking views and vibrant local culture. The lake is a popular destination for boat tours, hiking, and exploring traditional Mayan villages along its shores.

Fact 2: Tikal National Park

Tikal National Park is an ancient Mayan city and one of the largest archaeological sites in Central America. Located in the northern part of Guatemala, Tikal is famous for its impressive ruins, including towering pyramids and temples. It's set within a lush rainforest that is home to diverse wildlife, making it a fascinating destination for history buffs and nature lovers alike.

Fact 3: Antigua Guatemala

Antigua Guatemala is a beautifully preserved colonial city known for its charming cobblestone streets, historic architecture, and vibrant cultural scene. It offers visitors a glimpse into Guatemala's past with landmarks such as the Santa Catalina Arch, the Church of La Merced, and numerous colorful markets and cafes.

Fact 4: Semuc Champey

Semuc Champey is a natural wonder consisting of a series of turquoise limestone pools and cascading waterfalls situated in the Lanquín Caves region. The pools are formed by a river flowing beneath a natural bridge, creating a series of stunning, swimmable pools. It's a popular spot for adventure activities like tubing, hiking, and exploring nearby caves.

Fact 5: Chichicastenango Market

Chichicastenango Market is one of the largest and most vibrant indigenous markets in Guatemala. Located in the town of Chichicastenango, this market is famous for its colorful array of textiles, crafts, and traditional goods. Visitors can experience local culture, sample traditional foods, and purchase handmade items like woven textiles, pottery, and masks.

Chapter 2: Travel Tips

- Fact 6: Best Time to Visit

- Fact 7: Language and Communication

- Fact 8: Safety Tips

- Fact 9: Currency and Payment

- Fact 10: Local Cuisine

Fact 6: Best Time to Visit

The best time to visit Guatemala is during the dry season, which runs from November to April. This period offers pleasant weather with lower humidity and minimal rainfall, making it ideal for exploring outdoor attractions and participating in activities. The wet season, from May to October, can be rainy and humid, but it also brings lush green landscapes and fewer tourists.

Fact 7: Language and Communication

The official language of Guatemala is Spanish, but many indigenous languages are also spoken throughout the country. English is not widely spoken outside of tourist areas, so it's helpful to learn a few basic Spanish phrases or use a translation app. Communication in rural areas might be more challenging, so having a local guide or translator can enhance your experience.

Fact 8: Safety Tips

While Guatemala is generally safe for travelers, it's important to stay aware of your surroundings and take common-sense precautions. Avoid displaying valuable items, stay in well-lit and populated areas, and use reputable transportation services. It's also wise to keep up-to-date with travel advisories and follow local guidance regarding safety and health precautions.

Fact 9: Currency and Payment

The official currency in Guatemala is the Quetzal (GTQ). Credit and debit cards are widely accepted in major cities and tourist areas, but it's a good idea to carry some cash for smaller establishments and rural areas. ATMs are available in urban centers, and exchanging money at local banks or exchange offices is straightforward.

Fact 10: Local Cuisine

Guatemalan cuisine features a variety of flavors and dishes, often based on corn, beans, and rice. Popular dishes include Pepian (a rich, spicy stew), Kak'ik (a traditional turkey soup), and tamales. Street food is also a great way to experience local flavors, with options like pupusas (stuffed tortillas) and fresh fruit. Don't miss trying local coffee and chocolate, which are both renowned for their quality.

Chapter 3: Famous Cities

- Fact 11: Guatemala City

- Fact 12: Antigua Guatemala

- Fact 13: Quetzaltenango

- Fact 14: Flores

- Fact 15: Cobán

Fact 11: Songkran – The Water Festival

Guatemala City is the capital and largest city of Guatemala, serving as the country's political, cultural, and economic hub. It boasts a mix of modern skyscrapers and historic buildings, with attractions such as the National Palace, the Central Market, and the Popol Vuh Museum. The city is also known for its vibrant nightlife, diverse dining options, and bustling shopping districts.

Fact 12: Antigua Guatemala

Antigua Guatemala, often simply called Antigua, is a beautifully preserved colonial city renowned for its stunning architecture and historic charm. With its cobblestone streets, colorful buildings, and well-preserved churches like La Merced and the Santa Catalina Arch, Antigua is a popular destination for tourists interested in history and culture. The city also hosts lively markets, festivals, and cultural events.

Fact 13: Quetzaltenango

Quetzaltenango, also known as Xela, is Guatemala's second-largest city and a key cultural and educational center. The city is surrounded by scenic mountains and is known for its historic buildings, such as the Cathedral of Quetzaltenango and the Municipal Theater. Quetzaltenango is also a gateway to exploring nearby volcanoes and indigenous villages, making it a great base for adventure and cultural experiences.

Fact 14: Flores

Flores is a picturesque city located on an island in Lake Petén Itzá, known for its charming narrow streets and colonial-style buildings. As the gateway to Tikal National Park, Flores is a popular starting point for visitors exploring the ancient Mayan ruins. The city offers a relaxed atmosphere, with beautiful lake views, vibrant markets, and a range of dining and accommodation options.

Fact 15: Cobán

Cobán is a city located in the Verapaz region of Guatemala, known for its lush cloud forests and coffee plantations. The city is surrounded by natural beauty, including the nearby Semuc Champey and the stunning natural reserves like Biotopo del Quetzal. Cobán is also famous for its traditional Mayan culture and unique local crafts, making it a great destination for nature enthusiasts and cultural explorers.

Chapter 4: Culture and Traditions

- Fact 16: Traditional Festivals

- Fact 17: Unique Clothing and Textiles

- Fact 18: Traditional Music and Dance

- Fact 19: Local Crafts and Art

- Fact 20: Mayan Heritage

Fact 16: Traditional Festivals

Guatemala is known for its vibrant and colorful traditional festivals that reflect its rich cultural heritage. One of the most famous is the Semana Santa (Holy Week) in Antigua, featuring elaborate processions and dramatic religious ceremonies. Other notable festivals include the Festival of Rabin Ajau, which celebrates Mayan culture with traditional dances and ceremonies, and the Day of the Dead (Día de los Muertos), where families honor deceased loved ones with altars and offerings.

Fact 17: Unique Clothing and Textiles

Guatemalan clothing is renowned for its intricate and colorful textiles, often made by local Maya women. Traditional garments include the huipil, a hand-woven blouse, and the corte, a wrap-around skirt. These textiles are adorned with elaborate patterns and symbols representing various indigenous communities and their cultural identities. Each region has its own distinctive patterns and styles, making Guatemalan textiles highly valued for their craftsmanship and cultural significance.

Fact 18: Traditional Music and Dance

Guatemalan traditional music and dance are deeply rooted in Maya and Spanish influences. Music styles include marimba, a traditional xylophone-like instrument, and garífuna music, which features drum rhythms and call-and-response singing. Traditional dances, such as the Baile del Palo Volador (Dance of the Flying Pole) and the Danza del Venado (Deer Dance), are performed during festivals and cultural events.

Fact 19: Local Crafts and Art

Guatemalan artisans produce a wide range of crafts and art, including hand-woven textiles, intricate beadwork, and vibrant pottery. Traditional crafts often feature indigenous designs and techniques passed down through generations. Notable items include colorful worry dolls, which are used to alleviate stress. These crafts are typically sold in local markets and are celebrated for their quality and cultural significance.

Fact 20: Mayan Heritage

Guatemala is home to a rich Mayan heritage, evident in its archaeological sites and cultural celebrations. The ancient Maya left behind impressive ruins such as Tikal and El Mirador, showcasing their advanced knowledge of astronomy and architecture. Contemporary Maya communities continue to practice traditional customs, including their languages, rituals, and ceremonies.

Chapter 5: Wildlife and Nature

- Fact 21: Unique Animals of Guatemala

- Fact 22: Rainforests and Biodiversity

- Fact 23: Volcanoes and Mountains

- Fact 24: Rivers and Lakes

- Fact 25: National Parks

Fact 21: Unique Animals of Guatemala

Guatemala is home to a diverse range of unique wildlife. Among its notable species are the quetzal, Guatemala's national bird known for its vibrant plumage, and the jaguar, a powerful predator found in the rainforests. Other remarkable animals include the howler monkey, known for its distinctive calls, and the resplendent quetzal, which is considered one of the most beautiful birds in the world. The country's varied ecosystems support a rich array of animal life.

Fact 22: Rainforests and Biodiversity

Guatemala's rainforests are among the most biodiverse regions in the world, hosting a wide variety of flora and fauna. The Petén region, in particular, is renowned for its dense tropical forests, which provide habitat for numerous species, including exotic birds, mammals, and reptiles. These rainforests are crucial for maintaining ecological balance and are home to many endangered species, making them important for conservation efforts.

Fact 23: Volcanoes and Mountains

Guatemala is characterized by its dramatic volcanic landscape, featuring numerous active and dormant volcanoes. Among the most famous are Volcano Pacaya, which offers opportunities for lava viewing, and Volcano Atitlán, providing stunning views over Lake Atitlán. The country also boasts the Sierra de las Minas and the Cuchumatanes Mountains, which are notable for their rugged terrain and scenic beauty.

Fact 24: Rivers and Lakes

Guatemala's landscape is marked by several significant rivers and lakes. Lake Atitlán, one of the most picturesque lakes in the country, is surrounded by volcanic peaks and traditional Mayan villages. The Usumacinta River, one of Central America's largest rivers, flows through dense jungle and is crucial for local ecosystems. These water bodies are vital for both the environment and the communities living around them.

Fact 25: National Parks

Guatemala's national parks protect the country's natural beauty and biodiversity. Tikal National Park is famous for its ancient Mayan ruins and lush rainforest. Other notable parks include the Sierra de las Minas Biosphere Reserve, which conserves unique cloud forests, and Semuc Champey National Park, known for its stunning natural pools and waterfalls. These parks are essential for preserving Guatemala's natural heritage and providing opportunities for eco-tourism.

Chapter 6: History and Landmarks

- Fact 26: Ancient Mayan Ruins

- Fact 27: Historical Sites

- Fact 28: Colonial Architecture

- Fact 29: Important Historical Figures

- Fact 30: Independence Day

Fact 26: Ancient Mayan Ruins

Guatemala is renowned for its impressive ancient Mayan ruins, which offer a glimpse into the rich history of this ancient civilization. Notable sites include Tikal, with its towering pyramids and grand plazas, and El Mirador, known for its large architectural complexes and extensive ruins. These sites highlight the Maya's advanced knowledge of astronomy, engineering, and art.

Fact 27: Historical Sites

Beyond Mayan ruins, Guatemala has a range of historical sites that reflect its diverse past. The historic city of Antigua Guatemala, with its well-preserved colonial architecture and ruins of churches and monasteries, offers insights into the country's Spanish colonial era. Other significant sites include the ruins of Mixco Viejo, an ancient Maya city, and the historic town of Rabinal, known for its role in indigenous resistance and cultural preservation.

Fact 28: Colonial Architecture

Guatemala's colonial architecture is a testament to its Spanish colonial history. In cities like Antigua Guatemala, visitors can admire beautifully restored buildings with baroque facades, arched doorways, and ornate churches. Key examples include the Santa Catalina Arch, the Church of La Merced, and the Cathedral of Antigua. This architectural heritage reflects the artistic and cultural influences of the colonial period.

Fact 29: Important Historical Figures

Guatemala has been shaped by several important historical figures. One of the most notable is Miguel García Granados, who played a crucial role in Guatemala's independence from Spain. Another significant figure is José María Reina Barrios, a 19th-century president known for his modernization efforts. These individuals contributed to the shaping of Guatemala's political, social, and cultural landscape.

Fact 30: Independence Day

Guatemala's Independence Day is celebrated on September 15th each year. This day marks the country's independence from Spanish rule, achieved in 1821. The celebration includes parades, patriotic events, and cultural activities throughout the country. It is a significant national holiday that reflects Guatemala's journey to sovereignty and its rich cultural heritage.

Chapter 7: Food and Drink

- Fact 31: Traditional Dishes

- Fact 32: Popular Beverages

- Fact 33: Street Food

- Fact 34: Regional Specialties

- Fact 35: Cooking Ingredients

Fact 31: Traditional Dishes

Guatemalan cuisine is rich in traditional dishes that reflect the country's diverse cultural heritage. Some of the most iconic dishes include Pepián, a thick stew made with meat, vegetables, and spices, and Kak'ik, a traditional turkey soup with a distinct red broth. Tamales, made from corn dough filled with meat or vegetables and wrapped in banana leaves, are also a staple in Guatemalan households.

Fact 32: Popular Beverages

Popular beverages in Guatemala include Atol, a warm, thick drink made from corn, and Horchata, a sweet rice-based drink flavored with cinnamon. Coffee is also a major part of Guatemalan culture, as the country is known for producing some of the world's finest coffee beans. In rural areas, Fresco de Rosa de Jamaica, a hibiscus flower tea, is a refreshing and widely enjoyed drink.

Fact 33: Street Food

Guatemala's street food scene offers a variety of delicious and affordable options. Tostadas, crispy tortillas topped with beans, cheese, and salsa, are a popular choice. Other common street foods include Chuchitos, small tamales filled with meat or vegetables, and Elotes, grilled corn on the cob served with lime, salt, and chili powder. Street vendors also offer sweet treats like Rellenitos, plantains stuffed with black beans and sugar.

Fact 34: Regional Specialties

Different regions of Guatemala boast their own culinary specialties. In the highlands, Jocon, a green chicken stew made with cilantro and tomatillos, is a local favorite. The Pacific coast is known for its seafood dishes, such as Ceviche, made with fresh fish marinated in lime juice and mixed with tomatoes, onions, and cilantro. In the eastern region, Tapado, a seafood soup with coconut milk, is a popular dish with Afro-Caribbean influences.

Fact 35: Cooking Ingredients

Guatemalan cooking is characterized by the use of fresh, locally sourced ingredients. Corn is a staple ingredient, used in dishes like tortillas and tamales. Beans, particularly black beans, are another essential component of many meals. Fresh herbs and spices, such as cilantro, achiote, and allspice, add flavor to Guatemalan dishes. Chiles, both fresh and dried, are commonly used to add heat and depth to the country's vibrant cuisine.

Chapter 8: Sports and Recreation

- Fact 36: Popular Sports

- Fact 37: Outdoor Activities

- Fact 38: Local Teams and Athletes

- Fact 39: Festivals and Competitions

- Fact 40: Recreational Spots

Fact 36: Popular Sports

Soccer, known locally as fútbol, is the most popular sport in Guatemala, with passionate fans and local teams competing in leagues across the country. Basketball also enjoys a strong following, particularly in urban areas. In addition to these, traditional Mayan ball games, such as Pitz, continue to be played in some regions, reflecting the country's rich cultural heritage.

Fact 37: Outdoor Activities

Guatemala's diverse landscape offers a wide range of outdoor activities for adventure enthusiasts. Hiking is popular in the country's many mountains and volcanoes, with destinations like Pacaya and Acatenango offering breathtaking views. The country's rivers and lakes provide opportunities for kayaking, fishing, and swimming, while the lush rainforests are perfect for birdwatching and wildlife spotting.

Fact 38: Local Teams and Athletes

Guatemala has produced talented athletes who have gained recognition both nationally and internationally. Local soccer teams, such as CSD Municipal and Comunicaciones FC, have a strong following and compete in the country's top league. In addition to soccer, Guatemalan athletes have excelled in individual sports like badminton, with some earning medals in international competitions, showcasing the country's growing sports talent.

Fact 39: Festivals and Competitions

Sports and recreational festivals are an important part of Guatemalan culture. The Juegos Deportivos Nacionales (National Sports Games) is an annual event where athletes from across the country compete in various sports. Another unique competition is the Palo Volador, a traditional Mayan ritual involving acrobats who perform daring stunts from a tall pole, typically held during local festivals and celebrations.

Fact 40: Recreational Spots

Guatemala offers numerous recreational spots where locals and visitors can enjoy sports and leisure activities. Lake Atitlán is a popular destination for water sports like kayaking and paddleboarding. The beaches of Monterrico on the Pacific coast are ideal for surfing and beach volleyball. For those interested in hiking and climbing, the Sierra de las Minas and the volcanic highlands provide excellent trails and outdoor experiences.

Chapter 9: Education and Learning

- Fact 41: School System

- Fact 42: Educational Institutions

- Fact 43: Learning Resources

- Fact 44: Youth Programs

- Fact 45: Libraries and Museums

Fact 41: School System

Guatemala's school system is divided into three main levels: primary, secondary, and tertiary education. Primary education is compulsory and free, covering grades 1 through 6. After completing primary school, students can attend secondary school, which includes basic and diversified education, leading to vocational training or preparation for university. While education access has improved in recent years, challenges remain in rural areas where resources are limited.

Fact 42: Educational Institutions

Guatemala is home to a range of educational institutions, from public schools to private academies and universities. The country's oldest and most prestigious university, Universidad de San Carlos de Guatemala, was founded in 1676 and continues to be a leading institution for higher education. Other notable universities include Universidad del Valle de Guatemala and Universidad Francisco Marroquín, both known for their strong academic programs and research.

Fact 43: Learning Resources

Learning resources in Guatemala vary widely depending on the region. In urban areas, students have access to modern textbooks, libraries, and digital learning tools. In contrast, rural schools often rely on more basic materials and may face challenges like overcrowded classrooms and limited access to technology. Non-profit organizations and government programs are working to improve the availability of learning resources across the country.

Fact 44: Youth Programs

Youth programs play an essential role in supporting education and personal development in Guatemala. Many non-governmental organizations offer after-school programs that focus on academic support, life skills, and extracurricular activities such as sports and arts. These programs are especially important in rural and underserved communities, where they provide opportunities for young people to continue learning and stay engaged in positive activities outside of school.

Fact 45: Libraries and Museums

Libraries and museums in Guatemala serve as important centers for education and cultural preservation. The National Library of Guatemala in Guatemala City houses a vast collection of books, historical documents, and manuscripts. Museums offer educational exhibits on the country's rich history, art, and culture, providing valuable resources for students, researchers, and the general public.

Chapter 10: Famous Landmarks

- Fact 46: Temple I in Tikal

- Fact 47: Santa Catalina Arch

- Fact 48: El Mirador

- Fact 49: Iglesia de La Merced

- Fact 50: Cerro de la Cruz

Fact 46: Temple I in Tikal

Temple I, also known as the Temple of the Great Jaguar, is one of the most iconic structures in the ancient city of Tikal, located deep within the Guatemalan rainforest. This towering pyramid stands at approximately 47 meters (154 feet) tall and was built as a funerary temple for a Maya ruler. Its steep steps lead to a small chamber at the top, offering breathtaking views of the surrounding jungle. Tikal is celebrated for its significance as a major center of Maya civilization.

Fact 47: Santa Catalina Arch

The Santa Catalina Arch is one of the most recognizable landmarks in Antigua Guatemala. Built in the 17th century, the arch originally connected a convent to a school, allowing nuns to pass between the two buildings without having to go out onto the street. The arch frames a stunning view of the Agua Volcano in the distance and is a symbol of the city's rich colonial history.

Fact 48: El Mirador

El Mirador is an ancient Maya city located in the remote northern region of Guatemala, known for its massive pyramids and extensive network of causeways. The city's largest pyramid, La Danta, is one of the tallest and most voluminous structures in the ancient world, reaching a height of about 72 meters (236 feet). El Mirador is still being excavated, offering valuable insights into the early development of Maya civilization.

Fact 49: Iglesia de La Merced

Iglesia de La Merced is a stunning baroque-style church located in Antigua Guatemala. Built in the mid-18th century, the church is known for its elaborate yellow-and-white façade and intricate carvings. Inside, the church houses one of the largest fountains in Latin America, along with beautiful altars and religious art. Iglesia de La Merced remains an active place of worship and a key attraction for visitors to the city.

Fact 50: Cerro de la Cruz

Cerro de la Cruz, or Hill of the Cross, is a popular viewpoint overlooking the city of Antigua Guatemala. At the top of the hill stands a large stone cross, offering panoramic views of the city's colonial architecture, cobblestone streets, and the surrounding volcanoes. The short hike to the top is a favorite activity for tourists and locals alike, providing a serene escape with breathtaking scenery.

Chapter 11: Arts and Entertainment

- Fact 51: Traditional Art Forms

- Fact 52: Music and Dance

- Fact 53: Film and Theatre

- Fact 54: Popular Festivals

- Fact 55: Local Artists

Fact 51: Traditional Art Forms

Guatemala is known for its vibrant traditional art forms, deeply rooted in the country's indigenous cultures. One of the most famous is the creation of intricate textiles, which often feature bold colors and complex patterns representing different Maya communities. Another traditional art form is mask-making, with brightly painted wooden masks used in ceremonial dances and festivals, reflecting the rich cultural heritage of Guatemala.

Fact 52: Music and Dance

Music and dance are integral to Guatemalan culture, blending indigenous and Spanish influences. The marimba, a wooden percussion instrument similar to a xylophone, is considered the national instrument of Guatemala and is central to many traditional songs. Folk dances, such as the Dance of the Deer (Danza del Venado), are performed during festivals and special occasions, often featuring elaborate costumes and storytelling.

Fact 53: Film and Theatre

The Guatemalan film and theatre scene, though smaller than in some other countries, is a growing and vibrant part of the arts. Local filmmakers often focus on social issues, indigenous culture, and historical events. Theatre is also a popular form of entertainment, with performances ranging from traditional Maya stories to contemporary plays, often held in cultural centers and theatres in major cities.

Fact 54: Popular Festivals

Festivals in Guatemala are colorful celebrations filled with music, dance, and traditional rituals. One notable festival involves elaborate processions and intricately designed alfombras (carpets) made of colored sawdust, flowers, and other materials lining the streets. Another significant celebration features giant kites flown to honor the deceased. These festivals offer a unique insight into Guatemalan culture and traditions.

Fact 55: Local Artists

Guatemala is home to many talented local artists who draw inspiration from the country's landscapes, history, and cultures. Contemporary painters are known for their vibrant and expressive works, often depicting scenes of Guatemalan life and mythology. In addition to painters, many artisans create traditional crafts such as pottery, textiles, and jewelry, blending ancient techniques with modern designs. These artists play a vital role in preserving and promoting Guatemala's artistic heritage.

Chapter 12: Geography and Climate

- Fact 56: Diverse Landscapes

- Fact 57: Climate Zones

- Fact 58: Natural Disasters

- Fact 59: Conservation Efforts

- Fact 60: Unique Geographic Features

Fact 56: Diverse Landscapes

Guatemala features a wide range of landscapes, from lush rainforests and towering volcanoes to rolling highlands and arid plains. The country's diverse terrain includes the Sierra Madre mountain range, which extends through much of Guatemala, and the Petén region, known for its dense tropical forests. The Pacific coast offers beautiful beaches, while the Caribbean side features mangroves and coral reefs. This variety of landscapes supports a rich array of flora and fauna.

Fact 57: Climate Zones

Guatemala's climate varies by region and altitude. The lowland areas, such as the Petén region, experience a tropical climate with high temperatures and significant rainfall throughout the year. In contrast, the highland areas, including cities like Antigua Guatemala and Quetzaltenango, have a more temperate climate with cooler temperatures and distinct wet and dry seasons. The coastal regions typically have a tropical climate with high humidity and warm temperatures year-round.

Fact 58: Natural Disasters

Guatemala is prone to natural disasters due to its location on the Pacific Ring of Fire and its geological features. The country frequently experiences volcanic eruptions, with several active volcanoes like Fuego and Pacaya. Earthquakes are also a common occurrence, impacting both rural and urban areas. Additionally, Guatemala is susceptible to hurricanes and tropical storms, which can lead to flooding and landslides, particularly during the rainy season.

Fact 59: Conservation Efforts

Efforts to conserve Guatemala's natural environment are ongoing, focusing on protecting its unique ecosystems and endangered species. The country has established numerous protected areas and national parks to safeguard its biodiversity. Organizations and government initiatives work to address issues like deforestation, habitat loss, and wildlife poaching. Additionally, community-based conservation programs aim to involve local populations in preserving their natural resources.

Fact 60: Unique Geographic Features

Guatemala boasts several unique geographic features, including the stunning Lake Atitlán, renowned for its clear waters and picturesque scenery. The country is also home to impressive volcanic formations, such as the Volcano of Agua. Another notable feature is Semuc Champey, a natural limestone bridge with beautiful turquoise pools. These features contribute to Guatemala's rich natural heritage and attract visitors from around the world.

Chapter 13: Science and Technology

- Fact 61: Technological Innovations

- Fact 62: Scientific Research

- Fact 63: Technology in Education

- Fact 64: Environmental Initiatives

- Fact 65: Local Tech Companies

Fact 61: Technological Innovations

Guatemala has seen various technological innovations aimed at improving daily life and industry. Notable advancements include the development of mobile technology applications tailored for rural communities, such as agricultural management tools that help farmers optimize crop yields. Additionally, the country has seen growth in renewable energy technologies, such as solar power, which are being implemented to provide sustainable energy solutions in remote areas.

Fact 62: Scientific Research

Scientific research in Guatemala focuses on areas such as biodiversity, environmental conservation, and health. Researchers study the country's diverse ecosystems, including its unique flora and fauna, to better understand and protect its natural heritage. Health research addresses local issues like tropical diseases and nutritional deficiencies. Research institutions collaborate with international organizations to enhance their scientific capabilities and address pressing global challenges.

Fact 63: Technology in Education

Technology is increasingly being integrated into Guatemala's educational system to improve learning outcomes. Programs aim to provide students with access to digital tools and resources, including computers and educational software. Initiatives such as e-learning platforms and virtual classrooms help bridge the educational gap in rural areas, offering students new opportunities for learning and development.

Fact 64: Environmental Initiatives

Guatemala is involved in various environmental initiatives aimed at preserving its natural resources and combating climate change. Efforts include reforestation projects, which focus on planting trees to restore deforested areas and enhance biodiversity. Additionally, there are programs promoting sustainable agricultural practices and waste management solutions to reduce environmental impact and promote ecological balance.

Fact 65: Local Tech Companies

Several local tech companies in Guatemala are contributing to the country's growing technology sector. These companies are involved in diverse fields, including software development, IT services, and tech startups. They are working on projects that range from fintech solutions to health tech innovations, aiming to address both local and international market needs. These businesses are helping to drive technological progress and economic growth in the region.

Chapter 14: Economy and Industry

- Fact 66: Major Industries

- Fact 67: Economic Growth Sectors

- Fact 68: Export Goods

- Fact 69: Local Businesses

- Fact 70: Economic Challenges

Fact 66: Major Industries

Guatemala's economy is driven by several major industries, including agriculture, manufacturing, and tourism. Agriculture plays a crucial role, with products like coffee, sugar, bananas, and textiles being key exports. Manufacturing has expanded to include food processing, textiles, and apparel production. Tourism is also a growing industry, attracting visitors to the country's rich cultural heritage and natural beauty.

Fact 67: Economic Growth Sectors

Several sectors have shown significant economic growth in Guatemala, particularly in renewable energy and telecommunications.

Renewable energy projects, especially in solar and hydroelectric power, are gaining momentum as the country seeks to diversify its energy sources. The telecommunications sector has expanded rapidly, driven by increased mobile phone usage and internet penetration.

Fact 68: Export Goods

Guatemala is known for its diverse range of export goods, with agricultural products like coffee, bananas, and sugar among the most significant. Additionally, textiles and apparel are important export items, contributing to the country's manufacturing sector. Guatemala also exports fruits, vegetables, and cardamom, which is one of the country's unique and valuable agricultural products. These exports are vital for the country's economy, providing income and employment for many.

Fact 69: Local Businesses

Local businesses in Guatemala play a key role in the economy, ranging from small family-owned enterprises to larger corporations. Many are involved in agriculture, textiles, and crafts, producing goods for both domestic and international markets. Support for small and medium-sized enterprises (SMEs) is crucial for sustainable economic development in the country.

Fact 70: Economic Challenges

Despite its growing economy, Guatemala faces several economic challenges, including poverty, income inequality, and unemployment. Limited access to education and healthcare in rural areas hinders economic opportunities for many Guatemalans. Addressing these challenges requires coordinated efforts in policy-making, education, and investment to create a more inclusive and sustainable economy.

Chapter 15: Transportation

- Fact 71: Public Transport Options

- Fact 72: Road Networks

- Fact 73: Airports and Travel Hubs

- Fact 74: Cycling and Walking Paths

- Fact 75: Local Travel Tips

Fact 71: Public Transport Options

Guatemala offers various public transport options, including buses, minibusses, and tuk-tuks. The "chicken bus," a brightly painted former school bus, is a popular and affordable mode of transportation for locals and tourists. For longer distances, coach buses connect major cities, while tuk-tuks are commonly used for short trips within towns.

Fact 72: Road Networks

Guatemala's road network includes both well-maintained highways and rural roads. The Pan-American Highway runs through the country, connecting it to other parts of Central America. However, some roads, especially in remote areas, can be challenging due to rough terrain and limited maintenance. Despite these challenges, ongoing infrastructure projects aim to improve connectivity and road conditions across the country.

Fact 73: Airports and Travel Hubs

La Aurora International Airport in Guatemala City is the country's main gateway for international travelers. There are also smaller regional airports in cities like Flores and Quetzaltenango. These travel hubs provide access to various destinations within Guatemala and neighboring countries. Efforts are being made to expand and modernize these airports to accommodate increasing passenger traffic and enhance travel experiences.

Fact 74: Cycling and Walking Paths

In recent years, cycling and walking have gained popularity as alternative transportation modes in Guatemala. Cities like Antigua and Guatemala City have introduced cycling lanes and pedestrian-friendly areas, promoting healthier, more sustainable travel options. Efforts to improve infrastructure and safety for cyclists and pedestrians are also underway.

Fact 75: Local Travel Tips

When traveling in Guatemala, it's advisable to use official taxis or ride-sharing apps in urban areas for safety. In rural areas, it's best to travel during daylight and stay on well-known routes. Always carry small bills for transportation fares, and if you're unfamiliar with the area, consider hiring a local guide. Be cautious of your belongings and avoid displaying valuables. It's also a good idea to learn some basic Spanish phrases to help with communication and navigation.

Chapter 16: Environment and Conservation

- Fact 76: Conservation Efforts

- Fact 77: Endangered Species

- Fact 78: Protected Areas

- Fact 79: Environmental Policies

- Fact 80: Sustainable Practices

Fact 76: Conservation Efforts

Guatemala has made significant strides in conservation, focusing on protecting its diverse ecosystems and wildlife. Various organizations and government initiatives are involved in reforestation projects, wildlife protection programs, and community-based conservation efforts. These initiatives aim to address issues like deforestation, habitat destruction, and endangered species conservation.

Fact 77: Endangered Species

Guatemala is home to several endangered species, including the jaguar, the quetzal bird, and the howler monkey. Conservation programs work to protect these species through habitat preservation and anti-poaching measures. The preservation of their natural habitats is crucial for their survival and the overall health of Guatemala's biodiversity.

Fact 78: Protected Areas

The country has established numerous protected areas to conserve its natural heritage. Notable examples include the Sierra de las Minas Biosphere Reserve and the Maya Biosphere Reserve. These areas help safeguard critical habitats and promote biodiversity while offering opportunities for eco-tourism and environmental education.

Fact 79: Environmental Policies

Guatemala has implemented various environmental policies aimed at promoting sustainability and protecting natural resources. These policies focus on issues such as waste management, pollution control, and sustainable land use. Enforcement of these regulations is essential for addressing environmental challenges and ensuring long-term ecological health.

Fact 80: Sustainable Practices

Sustainable practices are increasingly being adopted in Guatemala, including organic farming, eco-friendly tourism, and renewable energy projects. These practices help reduce environmental impact and support the conservation of natural resources. Community involvement and awareness-raising are key to promoting and maintaining these sustainable practices.

Chapter 17: Language and Communication

- Fact 81: Official Languages

- Fact 82: Local Dialects

- Fact 83: Communication Etiquette

- Fact 84: Language Learning Resources

- Fact 85: Translation Tools

Fact 81: Official Languages

Guatemala's official language is Spanish, which is used in government, education, and daily communication. In addition to Spanish, there are 22 recognized Maya languages spoken by various indigenous communities throughout the country. These languages reflect Guatemala's rich cultural and linguistic diversity.

Fact 82: Local Dialects

In addition to Spanish, Guatemala is home to a variety of local dialects within the Maya languages. For example, K'iche', Q'eqchi', and Kaqchikel are among the most widely spoken Maya languages. Each dialect has its own unique linguistic features and is an integral part of the cultural identity of its speakers. Many of these languages are taught in local schools and used in community activities. Efforts to preserve and revitalize these languages are ongoing, supported by both governmental and non-governmental organizations.

Fact 83: Communication Etiquette

In Guatemala, communication etiquette is influenced by both Spanish and indigenous cultures. Politeness and respect are important, and it is common to use formal greetings and titles. When interacting with indigenous communities, showing respect for their traditions and using local language greetings can enhance communication and foster positive relationships.

Fact 84: Language Learning Resources

There are various resources available for learning both Spanish and Maya languages in Guatemala. Language schools, community centers, and online platforms offer courses and materials for learners of all levels. Additionally, immersion programs and language exchange opportunities provide practical experience in using these languages.

Fact 85: Translation Tools

For travelers and non-native speakers, translation tools can be very helpful. Smartphone apps and online translators offer support for Spanish and some Maya languages. While these tools can assist with basic communication, learning key phrases and cultural nuances can further enhance interactions and understanding. Additionally, engaging with local residents and practicing the language can provide valuable real-world experience and improve overall communication skills.

Chapter 18: Fun Facts and Trivia

- Fact 86: Interesting Historical Tidbits

- Fact 87: Quirky Local Customs

- Fact 88: Unique Festivals

- Fact 89: Surprising Discoveries

- Fact 90: Remarkable Geographical Features

Fact 86: Interesting Historical Tidbits

Guatemala is home to one of the most important archaeological sites of the Maya civilization: Tikal. This ancient city was a major political and cultural center during the Maya Classic period and features impressive pyramids and temples that continue to attract researchers and tourists alike. The site is also renowned for its well-preserved stelae and altars, which provide valuable insights into Maya history and culture.

Fact 87: Quirky Local Customs

One quirky custom in Guatemala is the celebration of the "Feria de la Candelaria," where locals dress up in elaborate costumes and masks to honor various saints and historical figures. This lively festival includes music, dance, and colorful parades, reflecting the country's rich blend of indigenous and colonial traditions.

Fact 88: Unique Festivals

The "Festival de los Barriletes Gigantes" in Santiago Sacatepéquez is a unique festival where giant kites are flown to honor deceased loved ones. These kites, which can be up to 20 feet wide, are intricately designed and represent various aspects of Guatemalan culture and mythology.

Fact 89: Surprising Discoveries

In 2018, researchers discovered a hidden network of ancient Maya cities in Guatemala using LiDAR technology. This discovery revealed previously unknown urban centers and complex road systems, shedding new light on the extent and sophistication of Maya civilization. The findings also highlighted the advanced infrastructure and planning that characterized the Maya cities, offering a deeper understanding of their societal organization.

Fact 90: Remarkable Geographical Features

Guatemala boasts a diverse range of geographical features. For example, Lake Atitlán is known for its stunning beauty and is surrounded by three volcanoes, offering breathtaking views and unique ecological diversity. Another remarkable feature is the Semuc Champey natural bridge, where turquoise pools are formed by the Cahabón River flowing through a limestone formation.

Chapter 19: Innovative Local Projects

- Fact 91: Community Development Programs

- Fact 92: Renewable Energy Initiatives

- Fact 93: Education and Technology Projects

- Fact 94: Environmental Conservation Efforts

- Fact 95: Social Entrepreneurship

Fact 91: Community Development Programs

Guatemala has several community development programs aimed at improving local living conditions. One notable initiative is the "Mi Familia Progresa" program, which provides financial assistance to families in need while encouraging them to invest in their children's education and healthcare. These programs focus on building local infrastructure, such as schools and health clinics, and supporting small-scale businesses.

Fact 92: Renewable Energy Initiatives

Guatemala is making strides in renewable energy to reduce its carbon footprint. The "Solar Rural" project is a significant example, where solar panels are installed in remote rural areas to provide electricity to communities that previously had no access to reliable power. This initiative not only improves the quality of life but also promotes sustainable energy use, helping to preserve Guatemala's natural resources.

Fact 93: Education and Technology Projects

To enhance educational opportunities, Guatemala has introduced "K'inal Antsetik", a program that integrates technology into classrooms across the country. This initiative provides schools with digital tools and resources, including tablets and computers, to improve the quality of education and bridge the digital divide. The project also offers training for teachers to effectively use technology in their teaching methods.

Fact 94: Environmental Conservation Efforts

Guatemala is committed to protecting its rich biodiversity through various environmental conservation projects. The "Defensores de la Naturaleza" organization leads efforts to protect endangered species and preserve natural habitats. Their work includes establishing protected areas, conducting wildlife surveys, and engaging local communities in conservation activities to ensure the sustainability of Guatemala's unique ecosystems.

Fact 95: Social Entrepreneurship

Social entrepreneurship is gaining momentum in Guatemala, with several innovative projects addressing social issues through business solutions. One such initiative is "FUNDAP", a nonprofit organization that supports small-scale entrepreneurs by providing training, funding, and resources to help them start and grow their businesses. These social enterprises aim to tackle challenges such as poverty and unemployment while promoting sustainable development.

Chapter 20: Future Prospects

- Fact 96: Technological Advancements

- Fact 97: Sustainable Development

- Fact 98: Educational Reforms

- Fact 99: Economic Growth

- Fact 100: Taiwan's Role in the Global Community

Fact 96: Technological Advancements

Guatemala is embracing technological advancements to drive future development. Initiatives such as the "GuateDigital" program aim to enhance digital infrastructure and increase internet access across the country. The government and private sector are investing in tech startups and innovation hubs to foster a tech-driven economy. Efforts are also focused on integrating technology into education and public services to improve efficiency and connectivity.

Fact 97: Sustainable Development

Sustainable development is a key focus for Guatemala's future. The country is working on various projects to promote environmental sustainability, including reforestation efforts and the promotion of eco-friendly agricultural practices. The "Plan Nacional de Desarrollo" includes strategies to balance economic growth with environmental protection, ensuring that development projects support long-term ecological health and resource management.

Fact 98: Educational Reforms

Educational reforms are being implemented to improve the quality of education in Guatemala. The "Educación para el Futuro" initiative aims to modernize the curriculum, incorporate technology in classrooms, and enhance teacher training. These reforms are designed to provide students with the skills needed for the 21st century and address disparities in educational access and quality across different regions.

Fact 99: Economic Growth

Guatemala is aiming for sustained economic growth by diversifying its economy and increasing foreign investment. Key areas of focus include boosting the tourism sector, supporting small and medium-sized enterprises (SMEs), and developing infrastructure projects. The "Estrategia de Crecimiento Inclusivo" outlines plans to create job opportunities, improve business environments, and enhance trade relations to drive economic prosperity.

Fact 100: Taiwan's Role in the Global Community

Taiwan's role in the global community has implications for Guatemala, especially in terms of trade and investment. Taiwan has been a supportive partner, providing aid and investment in various sectors, including technology and agriculture. The "Taiwan-Guatemala Partnership" includes collaboration on projects that promote economic development and technological innovation, reinforcing the bilateral relationship and contributing to Guatemala's future growth.

Conclusion

Congratulations, young explorers! You've discovered the wonders of "100 Amazing Facts About Guatemala." From ancient ruins to colorful markets, Guatemala is full of incredible surprises. We hope this book has sparked your curiosity and inspired you to learn more. Remember, the adventure never ends—keep exploring and let the magic of Guatemala stay with you!

Thank you!

Made in the USA
Las Vegas, NV
15 December 2024

14310602R00069